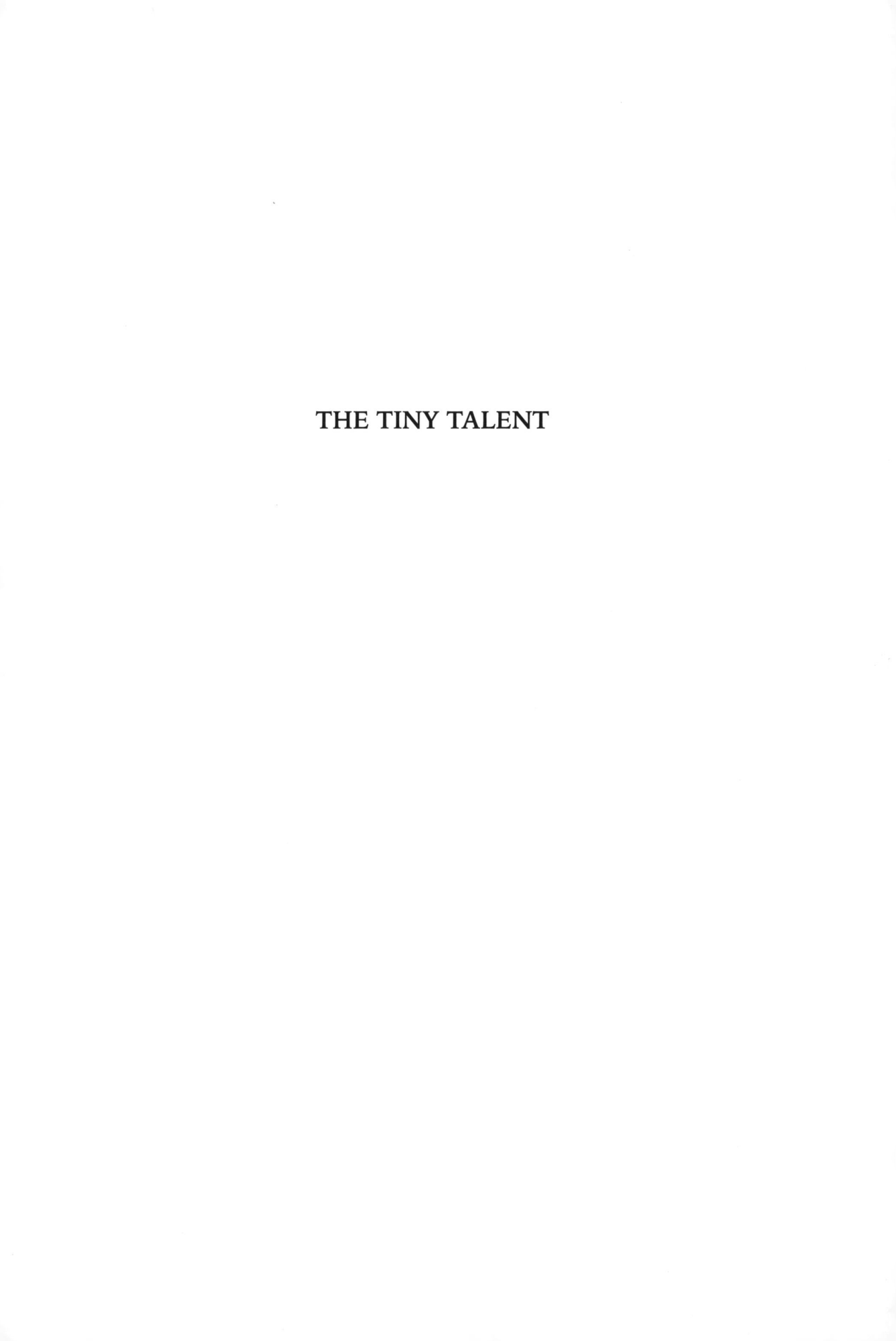

THE TINY TALENT

THE TINY TALENT

Selected Poems by Joan Ure

Selected and edited by Richie McCaffery and Alistair Peebles

With a foreword by Alasdair Gray

BRAE EDITIONS 2018

First published in 2018 by
Brae Editions
Buckquoy
Harray
Orkney
KW17 2JS
Scotland
UK

500 copies printed in Livingston by Ink on Paper

Designed by Alistair Peebles with Studio LR, Edinburgh

Cover: *Dark Images* (undated, detail) by Bet Low, courtesy of Lyon and Turnbull Auctioneers and The Bet Low Trust
Cover (inside, front and back): *Mousseline* (detail) by Amy Todman © 2018
Photograph of Elizabeth Clark/ Joan Ure © 1962 The Scotsman Publications Ltd

All Rights Reserved in text © 2018 the contributors: the Estate of Elizabeth Clark, Alasdair Gray, Richie McCaffery, Alistair Peebles

Brae Editions gratefully acknowledges the assistance of the following individuals and organisations: Stewart Conn; Eric MacDonald (including in recognition of the role played by Theatre Group Glasgow, and especially the late Robert Trotter, in supporting the work of Elizabeth Clark/ Joan Ure); Jan McDonald; Kenneth Roy; Scottish Poetry Library; Scottish Theatre Archive and Special Collections at Glasgow University Library; Christopher Small, for the Estate of Elizabeth Clark; Soulisquoy Printmakers, Orkney; Easton Wren; Frances Wren; and Creative Scotland.

ALBA | CHRUTHACHAIL

ISBN 978-1-907508-07-3

The Tiny Talent is distributed by Stromness Books and Prints,
1 Graham Place, Stromness, Orkney, KW16 3BY
+44 (0)1856 850565 | grahamplace1@hotmail.com

Copies are widely available, including from Good Press Gallery, 5 St Margaret's Place, Glasgow G1 5JY (goodpressgallery.co.uk); and from Lighthouse, 43-45 West Nicolson Street, Edinburgh, EH8 9DB (lighthousebookshop.com).

brae.editions@pm.me
@braeeditions

Contents

Foreword	1
TWO out of a DOZEN OPINIONATIONS	3
In Memoriam 1971	4
Mary	5
The Tiny Talent	6
GLASGOW, Easter 1968	8
Telephone Message	
From 'Words and Music'	9
More Dialled Tim	
HEADLINE!	10
Signal at Red	12
The Tree of Knowledge	13
To C.K. by Agony Column, *Glasgow Review*	14
Anger Flares Up Like a Match	15
We Must Eat a Bird for Christmas	16
Revelation – possibly	17
To a too modest friend	18
The thistle and me	19
SEX CHANGE (or The Optimist)	20
My Year for Being Resentful is Over	21
To Margaret on a Monday	22
THE FEMINIST	23
Answer on the Side Drum in 1963 to the Blast of the Trumpet in 1557, with Less than Respect	24
Editors' Notes and Acknowledgments	26

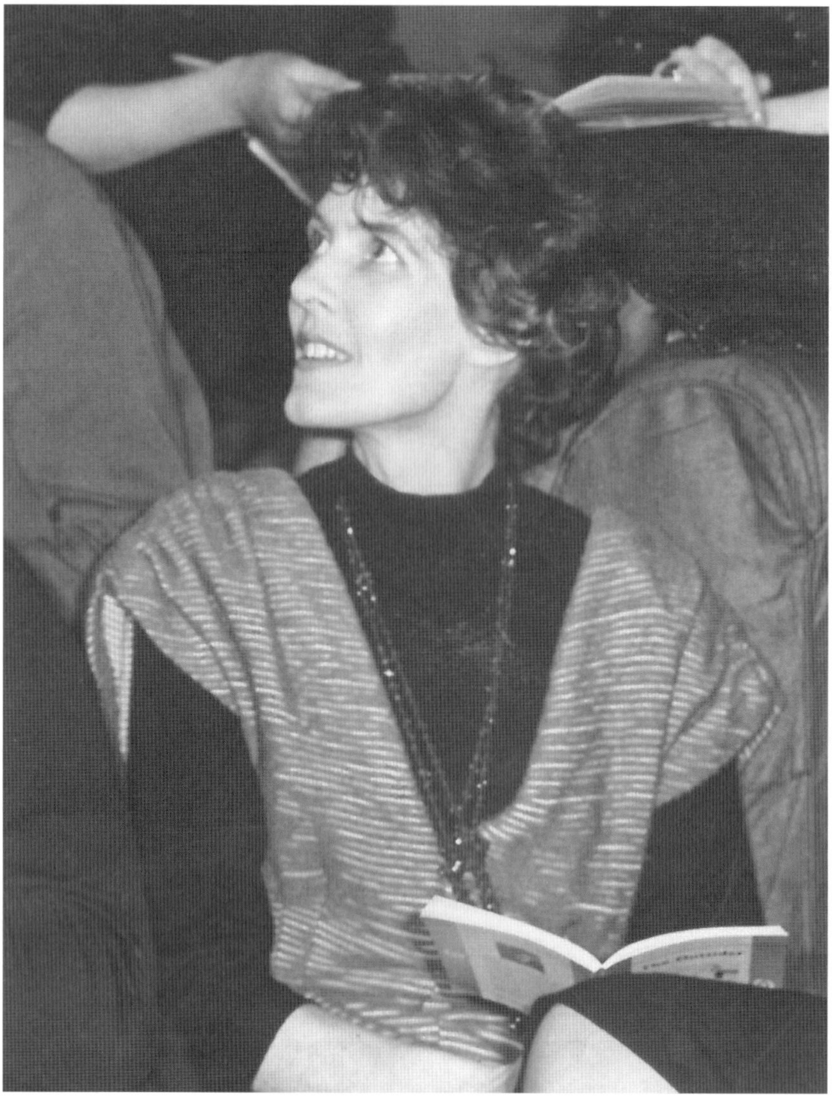

Foreword

I met this poet and playwright through my friend Archie Hind, when he and I were writing our first novels. This was long before we heard of Liz Lochhead, Tom Leonard, James Kelman and Agnes Owens, so in the 1960s we three were the only West Scottish writers, apart from some journalists, we much respected. Joan's baptismal name, Betty Carswell, had become Clark by marriage, and, on becoming a professional writer, she had chosen a pen-name to avoid embarrassing her relations. This Scottish tradition was observed by the authors of *Waverley, A Drunk Man Looks at the Thistle* and *Sunset Song*. The English middle class knows imagination can be an advantage, because other artistic daughters may find jobs in teaching, broadcasting or publishing, but poorer communities know artistic jobs are soonest lost when unemployment comes. Joan's plays had few productions because she worked in Scotland where hardly any theatres use local authors. Her plays were mostly short, witty, and managements distrust new writing that is cleverer than them. They think it may be stupid. Restoration dramatists, the Irish, and Noel Coward may write entertaining plays with polite, clearly reasoned speeches, but not the Scots. We are a violent people. Ok?

So, to get her work seen, Joan directed small productions performed by friends in an Edinburgh basement, sometimes acting in them herself. She made contact with amateur companies and worked hard, without pay, for organisations trying to change things, like the abortive Scottish Stage Company, and the more successful Scottish Society of Playwrights. Things are slightly better for local playwrights in Scotland today, and she is partly responsible for that, but the wear on her highly-strung nature was a punishing one. Most writers grow a surface to protect their nerves, rhinoceros hide or porcupine bristles or slippery suavity or facetious jollity. Joan Ure never did. What she showed you at any time was all there was of her, so even the company of close friends exhausted her after an hour or two. And, apart from one year when she got a Scottish Arts Council grant, she had always too little money. Her combination of intense drive and intense fragility led some colleagues to nickname her 'the iron butterfly'. Intellectually she was no butterfly and physically she was not iron. Instead of rusting and corroding like the rest of us, she drove to breaking point. Her last months were painful and lonely. She refused to depend on friends, she loathed hospitals, but she had to enter them. At last her lungs completely failed her.

Since her death in 1978, Joan's work has been unfairly neglected. I am glad to see this book of her poems.

Alasdair Gray

TWO out of a DOZEN OPINIONATIONS

1. What is bad
　about having to stay in Scotland
　from childhood
　　is that it unfits me now for getting out.
　　I am too barbaric to live
　　in a gentler land.
　　I'd be at the top of all their trees
　　in no time
　　chopping off their tender new branches
　　as we do here.
　　I am so used to subduing my gentler
　　inclinations.
　　There are no feminine virtues
　　that are useful here.

2. Where everybody is so serious
　and so competitive,
　who can afford to see any jokes but his own?
　All laughter here therefore
　is hollow
　as if there is no-one else in the room.
　The need for the ironic manner
　cannot be exaggerated.
　The pity that this is so
　breaks the heart eventually.
　Only hardened hearts
　go on beating in Scotland.
　It must be about time
　for a change.

In Memoriam 1971

Certain women. And some young boys.
Women with some uncertainties
but something they knew about
that made them need to say something.
Two of my father's sisters in childhood
and the first in my own lifetime –
Virginia Woolf and then,
oh in unbearably quick succession
my only sister. She died
but in her case they called it
a religious withdrawal
synchronous with late adolescence.
In a need for words there were
no words for, it seems to me now
it may have been impossible.
But I was too young then
I too took a long time growing up
and I was not aware of any need
not solved by tears or quickly effaced.
In fact supplied sooner than I was
ready. I conceived and then
I was married soon after.
I was lucky in those days and
it seems to me there were
other women whose troubles were
not to be solved by carrying the baby
even with the help of a wedding ring.
Sylvia Plath was not so simply satisfied.
Then last year the poet, Crae Ritchie,
my friend for not long enough,
a waver of flags for peace and joy.
This year, older, Stevie Smith.
In Scotland – or Ulster – she'd have
survived about half the time
by my stopwatch for I've been watching.
It used to be men who died for a cause
that other folk could hardly see. Now
it is women, rattling cans for aid to
the helpless, and young boys drugging
before they've even learned brutality?
I, personally, am getting scared
for me and my sons. And what if
I ever have a daughter?
Don't drown us out of the world:
it could be springtime.

Mary

And I won't remember this either?
That I am freed today to hope for you
that the girl at your hand gives you
pride of her beauty and all the rest
of it ditto and so on – honestly,
the ugliness in me gone for the moment.
It slid off because it has happened.
Taking courage to choose like tongs
I shall go to our places, will I?
I shall see the same people of course
because our interests seem parallel
but overlap – delicate distinction.
I shall see my face in mirrors and
mistake ten years' ageing for cause
when it was Us that aged and all
the rest of it ditto and so on.
At the intervals in the whiskies
I can dredge up this day's goodwill
after all my jealousy that stalked me
into hate and my hate that infected me
dirtier than my death was.

Ah, at last, not afraid of such language!

The Tiny Talent

There was this woman and she had this tiny talent.
I call it talent for things must have a name.
She had this talent that it happened to be death
to hide. She knew this empirically because, having,
the first time, tried to hide it, she
broke out in a rash.
But she was Scots and difficult to convince.
No worse for that perhaps but we shall see.
The rash, unfortunately, cleared up quite soon.
'It was no proof that I am hiding a talent',
she said, 'or I would have proof positive *now* and not
simply overnight'. She said 'I'll go and
hide my talent in another place.' She did good
works and other useful things. This time she
fell down in a faint! She could not blame good
works, so on she went being 'useful' everywhere
she could. Next time, she wakened in a sweat.
'The Devil', she said, 'The Great Deluder uses
ways like these and every one of them is to lead
a poor woman far astray.' And it happened that
this argument made it easier to live with her family
who had always been suspicious of what she, now
and then, saw as her talent, for doing something *else!*

'I'll hide the talent again!' she said, to her
mother and father, beginning to enjoy it as a game.
To do her justice – and her parents too – I should
explain that if she had been *sure* it was a talent –
if for instance it had appeared in a halo of gold –
she would not have hidden it anywhere. She'd
have rejoiced to do something with it, however small,
and however useless alas at the moment it seems to be;
for she was a serious girl with quite a primitive
racial memory which warned her all the time, as if
to some purpose which she could not divine, that
if you have a talent then it is Death to sit on it
for too long. In plainer terms, a talent
will *not* hatch out by being kept hidden and warm!

But how to blame her? How could she be sure,
when no-one had suspected her of talent but herself?
How to accuse her, when everything conspired to
suppress her need – talent or whatever it might be!
So she tried hiding it again, but this time with something
like finality about it – 'This time,' she said
'if something bad befalls me, I'll *believe* in it!'
Oh it was not – I may say – a difficult talent to hide!
It was very small and quiet and had passed unnoticed
everywhere, because of the – shall I say – noisier,
if not all the time larger, talents about.
This time she hid her talent well, with tears she couldnt
explain and had not expected anyway. She covered her talent
with flowers she couldnt afford to buy and felt guilty about.
Very soon it was that she coughed up the first very
beautiful gobbets of blood. There she saw the signs,
brilliant and red, if not exactly like a golden halo.
There it seemed, quite clear, the tiny talent she'd had.
Oh how that woman rejoiced! The thing was ridiculous.
No-one could alarm her with suggestions that the matter
was serious too.
'It was a genuine talent after all!' she told her mother
and father. They were weeping of course in the loving way
that mothers and fathers weep, over the fact that their children
have grown so far away all of a sudden.

This is a story that only seems sad at the end
but it is not sad because it is not a story but a
parable. It is good to know what they meant
when they talked of the talent, however small,
and that it is death to hide it. However late you
find it out, it is always good to know what it was
they meant, those few who're describing things that
can't be proved, but can be acted out
again and again.

GLASGOW, Easter 1968

I hate this city
and I reject it.
Love for it has tired
me out. The good
I expected when
I was a child has
been slaughtered at
every week's end.
Even a woman here
has to grow manly.
There is no gentle
place for a woman here.
It is a land of wee
hard men and all I
am wanted for is to
stand and cheer.
There is a service
to provide the
bandages.
I hate this city
and I reject it.

Telephone Message

("I have a cough; can't see you again this week")

I croak like a winter raven
but it's only the flesh
please distinguish
the flesh is, simply, inadequate
the words these hoarse sounds disguise
so successfully are the same
the blackbird effortlessly projected
at twenty five minutes to five
like a missile to the sky

from 'Words and Music'

Oh I am sick
to bloody death
from the gritty No
of a sour people
sick sick to death
And now I go
I sharpen my stainless skates
and I skate wild
on the frozen Yes
of my own joy
my joy, alone.
How about you?

(June 1965)

More Dialled Tim

This is a piece verbatim out of last Thursday's *Glasgow Herald*,
the back page, just above the Crossword.   I need my reading
glasses for this –
It's headed   "More Dialled Tim"
and I quote
       "Calls to the speaking clock
       telephone service totalled
       261,625,000
       in the year ending March 31,
       an increase of 8.63 per cent
       on the previous year"

Now I see that as a
Good Sign
More People Want to Know
Precisely
What Time it is.

HEADLINE! --- **THIS DAY THE PLAYWRIGHTS BURNED THE THEATRE DOWN!**

In the beginning
of this hopeful day
a woman is building
for herself a cage
set on the through
road of the city that
fronts the theatre.
She wears for warmth a
sedate sandwich board
that soberly states –
ALL I ASK IS FREEDOM
TO BE HEARD.
Several kindly souls
with bowls of soup
anxiously grow harsh
for she won't eat.
They try to persuade her
that she will catch her
death and – even worse –
that she makes here a
public exhibition of
herself for which –
as Equity entreats –
there is no fee.
Called out at last,
patient police point out,
disinterested, that she has
taken up her station at the
Cross and that is sacrilege
no less, beside the
gentlemen's lavatory too.
"The gentlemen have taken
to going without" the police
appeal at last to her
humanity.
"All I ask" she weeps, and
who could doubt her? "is
freedom to speak, freedom to
be heard."

"Speak up!" they say, over
the traffic noise and, leaving
her to it, wearying, turn away.
"THE PLAYWRIGHTS ARE ALL DOOMED!"
the woman wails, tearing at her hair
a true Cassandra, delighting in her
woe. Till gradually her mad eyes
light with hope – "THIS DAY THE
PLAYWRIGHTS BURNED THE THEATRE
DOWN!"   ("Explain! Explain! they
said, and she explained "They felt
the cold.   That's how it was" she
sighed.)
Oh somebody at this point
pulls the strings and her time
comes.   The happy woman is
washed and dressed and urged
under applause and lights to
say her say.   It is impossible
not to believe in her.
"Paranoia uncovers certain
truths" psychologists admit.
As her audience waits at last
attentively, she hesitates.
"Somewhere" she says, pulling
at a glove "somehow in the fight
I lost the very loving thing
I had to say."
And that is all.
Authorities, proved right again,
pronounce relief – "Well, no
more trouble there! We've
handled that quite well and
pass the port."
"The playwrights will not
burn the theatre down – not
yet" they murmur, relishing
their wine.

(December 1966)

Signal at Red

Nine years ago
or seven years
or no more than
three, and I
could see to-
day's joy that
lights me as a
prelude to love.
My excuse is I
was naive for a
long time, and
repetitively;
and your letter
is gently kind.
But I know, as a
working hypothe-
sis, that it is
from simple gra-
titude that now
I weep. It is
nine years too
late, or it may
be seven, or a
mere three that
I have remained
heartless, with
lips insensible
to the kiss of
love. However
I think I de-
cipher in your
biblical sim-
plicity your own
impersonal Love
living lonely in
its vacuum and
wanting no kiss?
If it is not so
then my signal
is flashing – no
healthy heart is
safe with me.

I am a cracked &
crooked mirror &
can give back no
reflection.
It is the heart
unduplicated,
not the mirror,
that will break.

The Tree of Knowledge

If, long before you had learned
to know the devil when you met him,
you had the poor taste to sup with him
not believing any of that nonsense about
using a long long spoon for the meal
– God help you! – you'll have
the devil to pay.
You'll be broken on the wheel,
over & over before he has
tired of you,
but then you'll be free.
Then you'll be Free.

To C.K.
by Agony Column, *Glasgow Review*

Unless you mean unique
I do not agree that people
are helluvan odd, however
life is and it is all
I can see so I am bloody
lonely alongside you.

We may not agree at all
but we are both in the
condition humane so
temporarily.

Can that be a comfort
when it can not be a help?
It is the silence
of the living dead
that damns me.

Anger Flares Up Like a Match

It is only by savaging you
the anonymous who read unknown
savaging in words of course –
I have no choice of weapons
in my philosophy –
only by belabouring you
because of Your Blindness
on this one page among other
politically useless pages
of dispensable paper
in a future that is
never existent
even then,

only this ranting frees me
so that I can love now

this unique man here
his irreplaceable woman and
the absurdity that is her child.

All blindly
blundering daily
wither their eternity.

In such stupidity
and beauty
they lose time
each day

as I do
I hope
too.

We Must Eat a Bird for Christmas

But out of doors
this noonday – for it is now
noonday and there is a bright sky
and the skeletons of trees trace
a lacy pattern between me and my neighbours,
my face-to-face, well-working neighbours
in the high flats back-to-back
face-to-face with me,
and downstairs at the kitchen window
eating the nuts we provide daily
there are twittering small birds –
certainly greenfinches
(I call them linnets)
and a great tit –
I saw him again this morning –
and sometimes, quite often, blue tits
like chorus girls, when the linnets allow.
And always sparrows waiting for what falls.
Ingenious city birds, sparrows, intelligent
of necessity.
And somewhere in our vicinity again this year
we seem to have – and I don't know just how –
come to deserve a Robin!
Its red breast is bared, divided
like a heart, or a pear if you're precise.
Somehow – I don't know how –
for it has all been terrible this year,
we have deserved a robin,
with its heart bared to the cold air.

Revelation – possibly

Have I ever seen anything as bright
on the yet bare branch of a tree
as that robin's stained pink breast?
 –   I doubt that I exaggerate it.
A solid bird at other seasons,
a sweet gay bird at Christmas,
is now this emblem of wounded passion
 –   Oh shout it, bird, don't sit silent!
The colour he wore sharp as a shield
in winter, a badge, a pseudonym merely,
betrayed none of this suffused pathos
 –   He was a bit of a hopping comic
Not quite absorbed in ranks of birds
wearing his ridiculous emblem, solitary,
unfitting signal on the drab of his brown,
now he over-reaches bird-sufficiency
 –   proclaim it!   Proclaim it!
Oh pink, oh pulsating, oh radiant breast
make some sign to announce yourself
or remain silent wearing such beauty
and when you go how will I find you?

Post Mortem

Around the felled tree
the men of logic hover –
      "It never was a robin, your dead bird
      Your bloody miracle was a mating chaffinch.
      Exalt its breast as a silent signal?   How absurd!
      The rationale is simple to discover
      We'll take the body to the lab and send you word."

(Easter 1966)

To a too modest friend

The crocuses are lovely.
No colour yet (just that
promise of it)
but they are taller.
They are aiming high.
Aiming towards the Spring.
What faith a crocus has!
It never doubts
that it is beautiful
and good and serves
some purpose.
And yet, if it set to
"measuring" and "comparing"
and losing faith, in fact,
how it would wilt!
Even a crocus knows
it has a right
to the care it was given.
Free.   Even a crocus.
Oh it's a sad thing
if all the faith in light
and the Spring is left
to crocuses!
I'm glad a crocus has
the sense to know itself
part of a shape which
may not always be just
but is beautiful.
It is the lack of justice
that leaves one
something to do.

The thistle and me

I grew a thistle this year.
I did not grow it exactly.
It chose my garden to grow itself in.
      But how I protected it!
It was I who cut back the blackcurrant bushes
and they are of use as everyone knows who
is in the least interested in dietetics –
because of the very high vitamin content.
      The thistle has grown to four foot
high.   It carries twenty-four purple plumes.
I had my photograph taken in colour beside it,
kneeling, the way people stand at a monument
beside James Hogg at Ettrick or Burns at Dumfries.
A young and coming poet can't resist it
      if he isn't too sophisticated.
To know that we have something in common,
in spite of appearances
I have gone on record, shoulder to spike
      with a thistle.

SEX CHANGE (or The Optimist)

My love cannot afford me
yet he won't let me go.
For years he has ignored me
successfully or so
it seemed to me
till lately when it seemed
I set him free
& now I find he'll take me
& yet can let me be.

My love & I were lovers
before our love began
because I was a woman
and he, my first, a man.
Mysterious to each other
as understanding grew
he becomes quite human
and I?   I wish I knew.

My love I give to girls now
Girls I now ask to stay
They are my new tomorrow
Boys I now send away
In the opening eyes of girls now
I see the future's dawn
I expected too much of boys once
Girls I now dote upon.

(March 1976)

My Year for Being Resentful is Over

My Year for being resentful is over
I only have to twist my arm
to prove it to myself.
It's true, it still seems more difficult
for me to get them to put on my very good
plays than it is for other people
whose plays are only so so.
It would be better to be secondrate
or if I'm secondrate anyway, it is obvious
that it would be better to be third class
for then I wouldnt have to convince
anybody that not understanding my stuff
on the page doesnt guarantee my superiority
and therefore is not causing an offence.
Oh, I'd forgotten – my year for being revengeful
is over: I am as mild as milk once again.
Being as mild as milk wasn't an act even.
I really find it more comfortable to
believe in Other People, to trust them
to grow up and learn,
to mend their ways and love me
as I've been loving them for such a long
time.   I really cannot live resentful
and revenge is getting at myself,
so I have to believe that there isnt
in Scotland a reactionary trend
that only a spitfire could penetrate.
I try to tell myself that
there are people who see my material
as a sort of balance, not a threat.
Surely the Scottish Soldier, the Scottish
policeman, the Scottish Jack tar
is not all there is in Scotland.
For if it is, we haven't got
very far
but it's not my year for being resentful.
It's my year for loving everyone again.

To Margaret on a Monday

I saw you from my window, Margaret.
I was watching the seagulls swooping the sky.
The seagulls, I was telling myself, know
today is a day for trying out the wingspan.
And then I saw you moving uphill
climbing a step at a time, alone.
Some young girls and boys
passed you, afraid
to offer help
in the face of so much courage.
They could not, yet, understand it.
An older man, moving slowly himself,
stopped as to have the privilege
of walking beside you.
He knew enough already to see
that he had a lot to learn from you.
I looked up again for the seagulls.
I did not need them anymore, though.
Their gliding and joy were, I could see –
without their assistance now –
no greater than your own. Man flies higher than any bird
and in spite of the force of gravity.
I would not have known, precisely,
what brought me to the front of the house
if I had not happened to see you,
going up the hill
as if it was easy.

THE FEMINIST

There was a time when I was even stupider,
I believed then that Strindberg, for instance, was
a man who hated women.   This was nonsense of course
but I was stupider and didn't know that then.
That is, I thought once that Strindberg did not love
me, for instance.   Now I know how much he loved
me.   Each time he lost me he replaced me oh
so quickly.   He could not feel alive without me.
So it is with me, now, except my actions are
different, being a woman.   And yet, do you know,
I have never demonstrated my love of a man so much
as now that I will state my discontents.
I never treated men so fully as my equals – at
least potentially – as now I do since I rebel
when they are careless of me although I love
them.   Until I spoke out loud and said You
are not Fair to me!   all I showed plainly enough
was my condescension.   Oh, my beloved!
You see I am trying to explain.   And that's the sign,
Strindberg discovered, because he loved and needed
love from women, that she is his equal and he cant
ignore her.   I cannot be silent now about
my disappointments because I cannot yet ignore
you, oh my darling, I shall have nothing
more to say.   Except to God, for instance.

Answer on the Side Drum in 1963 to the Blast of the Trumpet in 1557, with Less than Respect

John Knox needed Women
the way the old-fashioned God needed Satan
the way the Left needs the Tories
right up to this September day.
It's the radical's way to get started.
He finds a thing to get warmed up over
like a baby when she's teething
needs a bone ring for her play.
That wee preacher was broken, too shauchly
to have vigour in his sex appeal
He had to have those that hurt him
to get on with what he had to say.
I can afford to forgive him
He had nae ma advantages!
I can find a man that loves me
I dinna need Knox to agree

These wee gapes in the man's armour
are nae mair than his traumas showing.
They dinna invalidate him.
He can't invalidate me.
He was nineteen months in the galleys
It guarantees you won't like rowing
It does not mak siccar you ken aboot women
but you do ken aboot slavery.
In 1557 in England and Scotland
there were a pair of such weemin ruling
he had to challenge their authority
with its fine long pedigree.
I owe that man my education
I cant help whiles being glad of it
I know he meant the books for the boys
but now they have got to me.

In the Buik and in the struggle Knox discovered
thoughts about the conspiracy of silence.
It's sure he was temperamentally glad to believe
God had given him the Special Ee.
He was certainly ready to be bossy
like many of the rest of us
but he felt he had earned authority.

I don't know if a man can earn that
but he *had* paid in pain to be *free*.
I don't believe he'd have hurled
his hysterical arrows of scorn
on two or three wee wandered women,
except two had tried to silence him.
Mary of Guise was piously banning his sermons
frustrating that tongue and that talent!
And earlier he had to flee from Mary Tudor.
He had a mighty prating talent
and he made mistakes on his journey,
but he punctured dictatorial queenship
as an example for you and for me.

The truth is, once you open as a question
the authority, for a start, of the weemin –
although thon weemin were bonny queens
they could burn you then like a tree –
you get the hale notion of equality started!
He set a hale country readin the Buik
in the cottage, the farm and the castle;
each man's conscience became his own mystery
He challenged us with oor ain decision
happit in oor slowly conscious keeping.
He cant blast me doon noo wi his blethers
I ken fine *he's* no God for me.
But it's no just his mistakes that hiv scarred us
– except as we continue to make them,
we'd be better finding oor ain mistakes,
if mistakes there must always be.
It's four hundred years since Knox and his Blast
It would be a monstrous and vengeful woman
who would ding him doon this Sunday
without any great hope of his answer.

No, if Knox lived among us in the Sixties
he'd be worth his vote, his meat and potatoes
with the rest of us, for he earned it.
We could grant him *our* equality.

Editors' Notes and Acknowledgments

It will seem obvious to everyone who reads this pamphlet that as well as being a playwright, Joan Ure was undoubtedly also a poet. It would be obvious to all except perhaps one – if it's possible to imagine her reading it – Ure herself. In a letter of March 1963 to Christopher Small, literary editor of *The Glasgow Herald*, drama critic and supportive friend, she tells him:

> I don't write poems. I write pieces for acting. Sometimes I type them with irregularly shaped lines, but that's to help an actor read them, for the sake of the sense, but I don't write poems at all.

More cryptically, Ure once observed that even if she did write poems, they would be 'a failure – not intentionally, but because of the world'. Into this statement we must read Ure's threatened status as a Scottish woman writer, working in a climate evidently hostile to her talent, intellect and identity. In remarks such as these, we sense vividly Ure's frustration, but her rejection of the idea that her work could properly be described as poetry must be read in the context of that frustration: that things in life were regularly denied to her. Take, for instance, 'Answer on the Side Drum in 1963 to the Blast of the Trumpet in 1557, with Less than Respect'. This was originally written as a monologue to be delivered to a theatre audience, but in a letter of September 1963, again to Small, Ure reports having heard that an objection on religious grounds had led to its cancellation. The piece was then left languishing in an unpublished and unperformed limbo, where it has remained until now. Can it not also be considered a poem, if one of the core requirements of a poem is that it be memorable, musical speech? And, naturally, of her work that did make it into print, much of it is rightly to be found in the poetry section of the journal in which it appears.

If those remarks of hers suggest a keenly self-critical attitude, it is clear that Ure took her craft as a writer very seriously. Thus, in her 1968 essay on the soldier figure in Scottish culture for *Scottish International*, she claimed that 'I am a writer, a real writer […] I can't be bought off when it comes to the Word'. Earlier, in 1962, writing for *Scottish Field* under her married title of Elizabeth Clark (soon to be eclipsed professionally by her pen-name) she argued that an age that preferred newspapers and journalism to creative writing was one keen to 'hide real areas of human communication'. The job, for Ure, was to treasure and preserve the 'real' channels of human communication, as she saw them, through art: 'I believe in the creative writer […] I believe in language. I will not muck about with it'. As such, much of Ure's writing bridges the gap between drama, monologue, performance and poetry. Twenty-two items have been selected for publication here, and many more might have been included. Whether these are read aloud to an audience or silently by a single reader, they communicate no less as poetry than as glimpses into the character of her work as a playwright—and her distinctively lyrical and ironic voice is detectable in them all.

Just as Ure did not 'muck about' with language, the editors here, as far as is possible, have adhered faithfully to the original manuscript and typescript versions. Where there was an obvious spelling error, the correction has been made, but Ure's intended layout, punctuation, titling, and at times eccentric capitalisation of words and lines, have been retained. Dates of composition are given, where these are noted in the manuscripts.

Most of the poems came from Ure's sizeable archive held within the Scottish Theatre Archive, located at Glasgow University Library. The editors' thanks are due to the librarians and staff of its Special Collections department for their assistance, and similarly to the staff of the Scottish Poetry Library for help in sourcing print publications. Christopher Small, Ure's literary executor, is owed a large debt of gratitude for allowing this selection to be published for the first time. Frances Wren, Ure's daughter, whose helpful annotations can be found on a number of her mother's manuscripts in the archive, gave her warm approval to the production of this pamphlet. Thanks must also go to Alasdair Gray, not only for his foreword but also for his previous work on raising Ure's posthumous profile as a writer, and for working to preserve her literary remains. The publisher's own acknowledgments to these and other individuals and organisations are noted above.

The idea of seeking to publish a selection of Ure's poetry first arose in late 2017. It derived in part from an awareness that as well as being the occasion to celebrate the achievements of a number of other notable Scottish writers, and reawaken interest in their work, 2018 also marked Ure's own centenary, though one that at the time seemed likely to be overlooked. Beyond that, the circumstances that led to the suggestion of a collaboration – between an Orkney-based small publishing house, dormant for several years, and an editor then living in Ghent – might seem improbable. But as the ideas took shape, the encouragement we received, not least from those learning about Ure for the first time, confirmed our starting impression that as regards the wider appreciation of her work, it might indeed be 'about time/ for a change'. In her lifetime, apart from essays, prose pieces, poems, short plays and reviews in Scottish periodicals, Ure saw the publication of no more than one small booklet of her writing, *Two Plays*, brought out by Kenneth Roy in 1970. A later selection, *Five Short Plays*, edited by Christopher Small, appeared only posthumously, in a limited edition published by the Scottish Society of Playwrights (of which Ure was a founding member). Although magazines such as *Chapman* deserve praise, for first having brought to notice poems such as 'The Tiny Talent', and for striving to maintain interest more generally, no attempt has been made until now to gather together a broad range of Ure's poetry. Yet the work surely speaks no less forcefully today than when it was written. Its availability here, we hope, will further demonstrate, and help celebrate, the substantial achievements of a 'real writer'.

Poems in this selection that have previously been published:

'In Memoriam 1971' – *Scottish International* (November 1971).
'The Tiny Talent' – *Chapman 28/29* (Summer 1980). Subsequently published online in 2016 by *Keep Poems Alive International*.
'Glasgow, Easter 1968' – *Words 7* (undated, c. late 1970s). Subsequently collected in the (Hamish Whyte ed.) anthology *Mungo's Tongues: Glasgow Poems 1630-1990* (Edinburgh: Mainstream Publishing, 1993).
'Signal at Red' – *Scottish Poetry 1* (Edinburgh: Edinburgh University Press, 1966).
'To C.K. by Agony Column, *Glasgow Review*' – *The Glasgow Review* (Autumn 1964).
'Anger Flares Up Like a Match' – *The Glasgow Review* (Winter 1964/5).
Press clippings exist in Ure's archives for both 'To Margaret on a Monday' and 'We Must Eat a Bird for Christmas'. These were probably taken from *The Glasgow Herald*.